CONTENTS

Title Page	
Legal Notes	1
Why You Should Read This Book	3
How to Read This Book	6
Useful Information for your benefit	7
Chapter 1 - Develop the Habit of Saving Money in Everyday Life	8
General Ways To Save Money	9
Some Tips to save water usage at home	26
Saving Money whenever you are Calling, - For Local as well as for Overseas calls	27
Related to Habits	29
Chapter 2 - Saving Money While at Home/Office	32
Chapter 3 - Related to Earnings, Savings and Investments	36
Chapter 4 - Related to Debt, Loans, Credit Cards	41
Chapter 5 - When Partying/Going out for Entertainment	43
Chapter 6 - Related to Vehicles/Transportation	46
Money Saving Tips while Buying a New Car	47
General Money Saving Tips for Vehicles/Transportation	50
Chapter 7 - Saving Money while Travelling/Going on a Vacation	53

Saving Money while Booking Hotels and Flight Tickets	54
Ending for now	58
Can I Ask a Small Favor?	59
Would you like to get the latest information about my new and upcoming releases?	60
About the Author	61

START SAVING MONEY RIGHT NOW

125 Practical Ways To Save Money, *Learn Each Of Them in 5 Minutes or Less. And Have a Secure Financial Future.*

By: - ROCKY KUMAR
Copyright © 2019

Subscribe for all the Latest Updates about New Releases at:
www.PassionateIdeas.net

LEGAL NOTES

Start Saving Money Right Now

125 Practical Ways to Save Money, Learn each of them in 5 Minutes Or Less. And have a Secure Financial Future.

Copyright © 2019 by ROCKY KUMAR.

All Rights Reserved

No part of this publication may be reproduced, distributed, or transmitted in any form or by any means, mechanical or electronic, including photocopying or recording, or stored in a database or retrieval system, or transmitted by email without the prior written permission of the author. This copy is intended for the purchaser of this book only, or sharing as permitted by your book vendor.

Disclaimer

Please note that this book is for entertainment purposes only. The views expressed are those of the author alone, and should not be taken as expert instruction or commands. The reader is responsible for his or her own actions.

While all reasonable efforts have been made to verify the information provided in this book, neither the author nor the publisher assumes any responsibility for any unintentional errors, omissions, or for the contrary interpretations of the subject matter herein, or for any loss incurred as a consequence of use/application of any of the contents of this book. This book does not make any guarantee of results and is not intended for use as any source of advice.

Adherence to all applicable laws and regulations, for domestic as well as international regions, is the sole responsibility of the purchaser or reader. Neither the author nor the publisher assumes any responsibility or liability whatsoever on behalf of the purchaser or reader of these materials.

Any perceived slight of any individual/organization is purely unintentional.

The author may earn a commission if the reader purchases something or joins a program using a link anywhere in this document, or the websites referenced. The reader should do his/her own research before making any purchase online/offline.

WHY YOU SHOULD READ THIS BOOK

In these uncertain economic times, everybody needs to curtail their expenses and save as much money as they can. This is most essential for both individuals as well as for businesses.

We cannot predict the economic future, but we can surely try our best today, to spend responsibly, cut down on the unnecessary items, and save as much as we reasonably can, so that we are assured of at least one thing – "that we will definitely have money when we need it".

By saving money on a regular basis, we can have:-

- A Stress Free Life in the Present Times.

- Future Financial Security.

- We would not have to worry a lot, regarding any slowdown in economy, Or any economic recession.

Also, most of the times, we are bothered by stressful money related thoughts. For example:-

- Why does my Salary Finish, before the month ends? How to save money from monthly salary?

- My work requires me to Travel a lot, especially Overseas Travel. How to start saving money on travelling expenses? Also, how can I save money while going on a vacation?

- I want to Control my Spending Habits, and Save some Money, but how to do it?

- Why do I Overspend, all the time, at Every Occasion? How can I Control it?

- How to spend less and how to save money in bank?

- What are some of the best ways to save money?

- What should I do to Save My Money, starting Right Now?

- Etc.

Like me, if you are also concerned by some/all of these questions, (and maybe other matters related to saving money), then this short book of practical ideas might just be perfect for you.

This book has a list of 125 Practical Ideas, on how to start saving money right now.

These ideas are very easy to implement on a daily basis, in order to develop good habits of saving money. Thus, one can hope to become a money saving expert in the long run.

Some Important things, which you can learn through this book, are:-

- How to Manage your Existing Money/Existing Income.

- How to Save Money while Shopping (For Personal as well as for Business requirements).

- Focusing on Goals and Investments as an incentive to save money.

- How to Save Money on Communication/Phone Expenses (Personal as well as Business).

- How to Use Credit Cards optimally.

- Saving Money, when partying/going out for Entertainment.

- Ways to save money when travelling/Going for a Vacation.

- How to Save Money, when purchasing a New Car (and also save money on its maintenance and on insurance).

- And a Whole Lot More......

These 125 money saving tips would be useful for all working professionals, traveling salesmen, students as well as for housewives.

So, go ahead, enjoy reading this book, and hopefully you will find some Ideas to be good enough to apply in your daily lives, and can derive the maximum benefit out of them.

HOW TO READ THIS BOOK

This is a book of **"IDEAS"**.

It presents a lot of Ideas, in a simple, easy to read, list format.

There is no particular way to read this book. You can either start from the beginning or you may pick any chapter as you like.

The more important thing is to actually "Realize", how these ideas can be beneficial in your everyday life. Make a habit of implementing those ideas which you find good, and feel free to discard the rest.

Keep this book available, if you want to refresh your memory anytime, or want to think of some new ideas to save money.

Happy Reading…..

USEFUL INFORMATION FOR YOUR BENEFIT

"Thank you" for purchasing this book.

I write a lot about Productivity and Financial habits, and am currently in the process of finalizing a few more books for publishing.

As a token of my appreciation; I would like to provide you more useful information about the "Release" of my further books.

You can click the below link to SUBSCRIBE to my Blog, and get timely updates on future releases.

Happy Reading.....

ROCKY KUMAR

Subscribe Here: - www.PassionateIdeas.net

CHAPTER 1 - DEVELOP THE HABIT OF SAVING MONEY IN EVERYDAY LIFE

GENERAL WAYS TO SAVE MONEY

1) You can start by Managing your Money/Existing Income, in a structured way.

- Make a Budget and Stick to it.... Period.

In the beginning of every month, focus on allocating money from your monthly income, for different areas:-

a) First of All - Allocate money for the most essential items as well as for the routine expenses – Like Food, Household Goods, Electricity, Gas, Tuition fees, Clothes, Monthly EMI for Loan, Credit Cards, etc.

b) Then, from the remaining amount, allocate some amount for your savings/investments. (This amount can be flexible, depending upon your long term goals and priorities).

c) Then, out of the remaining amount, use some money for entertainment purposes (going out for dinners, movies etc.).

d) Spend on Luxuries in the end (Like – going for an expensive vacation, purchasing costly gadgets, buying a new vehicle etc.).

By following this structured approach every month, you would be able to manage your expenses, as well as regularly contribute some amount to your savings account, (and this would eventually add up to be a substantial sum in the long term).

2) Track your Expenses/Record your Expenses.

For doing this easily, you can download any popular app on your mobile, or you can create an excel spreadsheet on your computer. Making such a list might take some time (maybe a week, or even a month), but this effort would help you a lot in the long run.

Track your expenses for a few months, and you will have a fairly good idea of various areas, where your money is being spent.

This will help you to identify the non-essential expenses from the essential ones, and then, you can slowly plan to stop purchasing/cutting down on the non-essential items, and focusing only on the essential items. Thus, you can start saving money in the process.

Furthermore, after a few months, you would also know the average amount of money, which you are spending in each area. For Example:-

a) Average amount spent on Fuel every month.

b) Average amount spent on Groceries.

c) Average amount spent Eating out, etc.

Once you have an idea of the average amounts, then budgeting becomes easier, and then, you can also easily decide upon the amount to be saved every month.

3) Have a Weekly/Monthly Savings goal, and stick to it.

In fact, it is one of the simplest ways to save money.

You can start with any amount you are comfortable with. Say $10 per week, $10 per month, or even or $100 per month.

The key is to be disciplined and to maintain the saving frequency as well as the amount.

(In the beginning, it might seem like a very small amount, but trust me - over a period of time, you would be able to accumulate a considerable sum of money in your savings account).

4) Got Loose Change?

Many a times, while shopping, we are left with some loose change/coins. When we reach home, then we take out these coins and keep it in some drawer/cupboard, from where we hope to retrieve them later on, whenever we need them.

It might happen that over a period of time, we have lots of different places/drawers in our home, where we have kept some loose coins now and then (and thus all of them are not kept together). So, when we really need those coins, then we are not able to find all of them at a short notice. It might also happen that they get lost during cleaning, or when you are shifting your stuff from one place to another.

The better way is to keep all loose coins/change in a separate box, and when you have lots of it, then you can get it exchanged for bigger notes, or can directly deposit them in your bank.

5) Furthermore, **at the end of every day**, check your purse/pockets for any loose change, and keep it in the separate box, for future use. This will ensure that they are kept safely and the possibility of losing them is minimized.

6) Save Money by Avoiding the Television.

By reducing the time spent on watching the T.V, you can have a lot of benefits, like:-

a) The Electricity Bill would be reduced (Fewer expenses translate to saving money).

b) You would have "Reduced Exposure" to Advertisements for products, which you might not need.

While watching any program, you might also watch an advertisement for the latest TV or Electronic gadget and might be tempted to buy it, whereas actually there was no "Real Need" for the same.

Thus, watching less TV indirectly helps you to save money in the long term.

In case, there is a definite, "Real Need", for any particular item (TV/Other electronic gadget/any other item), then you should definitely go ahead and purchase the same, else you can save the money for future use.

c) You would have more time available to indulge in other activities (For example – you can invest the time in running a Part time business/Working in a part time job/Learning something new/ Meeting with friends).

d) Furthermore, watching less TV is also good for the eyes.

7) Do a review of all the TV channels which you watch.

Out of the various channels which are included in your monthly cable subscription, keep those channels which you love to watch and prefer to remove the remaining channels from the subscription. In this way, you would be paying only for the channels/programs, which you want to watch, and thus save some money in the process.

8) Negotiate for Better Offers/Rewards/Discounts, wherever you can.

This can help you to save money in a lot of avenues. For example, you can start with:-

- Existing Cable service provider (for Lower subscription rates),

- Existing Mobile services provider (for Lesser Monthly bills),

- Existing Credit Card Issuer (For Rewards as well as Reduced Rates of Interest),

- Etc.

Start by making a list of all the possible areas, where you can negotiate for better savings. In some cases, the list can be become very long and thus, you can have numerous opportunities to save money in the long term. Also, there is no harm in requesting your existing service provider for discounts. They might be having some better offers/discounted schemes, which they can offer to you.

9) In Addition to the above, - whenever you are signing up for a new service, and it has some sort of "Initial Sign-Up Fees", then you can always request for that fees to be waived off. You never know, you might be lucky and thus can save some money. So, what's the harm in trying?

10) Also, your subscription provider might be offering **a host of add-ons along with your main subscription**, and charges for those add-ons are also included in your monthly/yearly bills.

Most of the times, one does not check these incremental amounts in the bill. But, over the years, it can add up to a huge amount.

Do make it a point to check your bills thoroughly and see if you really need those extra services. In case you really need those add-ons, then it is fine. If not, then you can request to get them removed from your bills.

By removing the non-essentials from your monthly/yearly billed amounts, you would be able to reduce your expenses and thus save some money in the process.

11) Pay all your Bills on Time.

Sometimes, we forget to pay our bills before the due date and this can lead to extra penalties/fess/interest being charged on the total bill amount. Some examples can be of:-

- Credit Card Bills (The interest charged on outstanding payments can be too high),

- Electricity Bills,

- Mobile Bills,

- Etc.

Since late fees/charges are an unnecessary expense, so make sure to pay all your bills on time, and thus save money, by avoiding any kind of Late Payment charges.

12) Develop the Habit of making all Bill Payments Online. When we have the option as well as convenience of paying all our bills online, while sitting at home/office, then we should surely utilize the same and save our valuable time as well as money.

To make a trip to the respective payment counter/office, one needs to take out his vehicle (fuel cost), as well as set aside considerable amount of time. Both of these are an expense, which can be avoided by going online.

Furthermore, online payments are done instantly, "Receipts" are generated immediately and the corresponding "Entries" also reflect in our bank account at the same time. So, we don't have to wait for the payment to be debited from our account and get deposited in the biller's account.

13) Make a List of all the Subscriptions you have.

From this list, evaluate which subscriptions are definitely needed. Keep only those essential subscriptions, and cancel the rest.

Examples can be of:-

- Magazine subscriptions (Online/Offline),

- Gym and Club Memberships,

- Newspapers,

- Etc.

In some cases, the list can be become very long. Thus, by removing the non-essential subscriptions from your expense list, you can have numerous opportunities to save money in the long term.

14) Consider Unchecking the Auto Renewal option, when you are shopping via Credit Cards.

When we purchase any subscription online via credit card, there is an option of Auto-Renewal of the subscription on a monthly/yearly basis. It is better to opt for One-Time Purchase, as compared to automatic renewal. In this way, whenever the renewal comes up, then you can again consider, whether you want to continue or not. In case, the subscription/service is essential, then by all means, you should go for the renewal, else you can save some money by not renewing the same.

15) Another good habit is - Not to store Credit Card Numbers in various online accounts.

It is a very convenient to store the credit card numbers in your online account and then you can purchase anything in a few clicks, without bothering to fill in the payment details every time. But, consider this - If you do not store the card details, then whenever you shop, then you have to do the "Extra work" of getting out your credit card from your wallet and again fill in all the required details. Although this is quite cumbersome, as you have to type-in the details again and again, but at the time of purchase you can once again think about whether you really need to buy that particular item, or not. If it is absolutely required, then do go ahead and purchase, otherwise you can save some money.

16) Whenever you go out for Shopping, First make a List at Home, and then -- Stick to it.

Don't do impulse shopping. Buy only the things on your Pre-defined list.

Making a list will have 2 advantages:-

Firstly, when you are making the shopping list, then you are already evaluating each item as essential/non-essential. This activity itself removes most of the items from being included in the list.

Making a list would ensure that you purchase only those items, which you need, which are most essential, which you have already accounted for in your budget. Thus, you are less likely to overspend.

Secondly, you would not forget anything, and will have to go to the store only once. Thus, you can complete your entire shopping in one trip only.

In case, you do not have a written down list, then after completing your purchasing and reaching home, you might realize that some essential items have been left out. In that case you might have to go to the store once more, which involves additional time, energy, as well as money (as you have to put fuel in your car).

17) Try out New Grocery Stores/Shopping Malls/Apps, etc. (for Better Deals and Discounts).

a) Start by checking the local newspaper for deals/discounts on the items, which you regularly purchase.

b) Consider installing an App on your mobile, which provides daily/weekly deals for general household as well as other items.

You might get lucky and find some Great Promotions going on/ Heavy Discounts being offered at some stores, for certain items of your interest. Thus, you would be able to save money in the process.

Also, check if the store/seller is providing home delivery for free. In this way, you can save both time as well as money.

18) Be on the Lookout for Free Customer Rewards Programs/ Cash back Offers/Discount Offers.

Every business needs repeat customers and the shopping stores generally offer some extra privileges for regular customers. So, next time you go shopping, do enquire, if the store has a customer rewards program, and "Sign up" for it. You are anyways going to buy stuff from there, and if you can also avail of some cash back offers, attractive discounts, or any other benefits, then it would surely help you to save some money.

Some stores might also be offering exclusive deals for customers, who have enrolled in specific programs. Check the eligibility for such programs and if you can enroll in them.

Also, if the store has an App, then Install it on your mobile for regular updates/Subscribe to their newsletters.

19) For Non-Perishable Household items, try to purchase in Bulk, whenever possible, and do negotiate while purchasing.

Some examples of non-perishable items can be:-

- Washing Powder,

- Soap,

- Tooth Brushes,

- Cleaning Cloths,

- Tissue Papers,

- Etc.

Bulk Purchasing of Non-perishable items would have 2 advantages:-

Firstly, since the shelf life of such products is more, so you can store them for longer periods and use them, whenever required.

The second advantage is that - buying in bulk helps to get a better discount from the store, and it also reduces the overall cost per usage. Thus, it helps to save money.

Additionally, do check out for any Promotional offers going on, which can again be beneficial.

20) A similar strategy can be applied whenever you are purchasing Business goods, for example - office stationery (paper, pens, pencils etc.).

Here also, we can plan to buy in bulk, and negotiate for a better price for each item.

21) Concentrate on the timing of purchase, so that the probability of getting discounts is higher.

- For example – purchasing during the "End of season sales".

- For next year's summer clothes, you can plan to purchase towards the end of summer season of the current year.

- Similarly, for next year's winter's clothes, jackets etc., you can plan to purchase towards the end of winter season of the current year.

- Etc.

Retailers want to clear the current year's inventory, so the discounts offered on certain merchandise can be substantial during the "End of Season sales". This is a good opportunity to save a lot of money, by buying quality products at discounted prices.

Also, during major Festivals/Holiday season also, many retailers offer Discounts/Attractive offers. So, this is also a nice opportunity to buy at good prices.

22) An Important addition to the above point is - You should go for shopping, only when you genuinely need something, and not because there is a sale going on.

Impulsive buying during sales would not help to save money. Rather, you would end up buying things, which you probably don't need.

The Important thing is to – First check your "shopping list" and then decide whether to purchase or not.

23) Before buying anything expensive, do wait for some time to contemplate (and also discuss the same with your family and friends).

Sometimes, one has the urge to buy a particular thing - Maybe the expensive/latest mobile, laptop, car, fashionable clothes etc., But if we wait for some time, and think over it, and maybe even discuss it with our near and dear ones, then we can realize - whether it is a necessity, or simply an urge.

In case, you realize that it is a necessity, then, you can proceed ahead and buy it, else you can save money for some other necessity later on.

So, having a "Cooling off" period, before purchasing expensive things can sometimes help you to save money.

24) Concentrate on buying only those items, which you "Need" and Sell those items, which you Don't Need.

This is related to the point of List building, to keep expenses in check.

Make a list of the things which you need, and then buy only those. This will help you to save money in the long run.

Also, if you have any stuff at home, which you do not need, then why not sell it online/offline, to make some extra money.

25) This point is again related to List building for managing your finances.

Try to visit Yard sales, and look out for items, which are on your list to be purchased. See if you can get some great deals for those items.

Just make sure not to buy those things, which you do not require. As mentioned earlier, impulsive buying during any sales would not help to save money. Rather, you would end up spending money to buy those things, which you probably don't need.

26) Can you consider purchasing used items/second hand items?

For Example - Consider buying a second hand car, which can save you a lot of money.

Items like clothing, mobiles, home appliances, even vehicles, can cost a lot less when they are bought second hand.

You just need to shop around for good deals for the items of your interest, do the due diligence, and then purchase.

27) Is it possible to repair Old Clothes?

If there is a minor tear/damage in the clothes, then do not throw it away. Check, if it can be repaired. One can save a lot of money by doing some minor repair/patchwork on old clothes as compared to buying new ones.

28) When shopping for clothes, do check online also.

Sometimes, the stores might be having some promotional offers for online shoppers/App only deals, or having some exclusive online deals. Just check around on various websites. You might be able to get the clothes as per your preference and also save some money in the process.

29) Similarly, whenever you need to purchase medicines, then

Compare Prices at various pharmacies/supermarkets, as the cost can vary from one pharmacy to another.

30) Prefer to make your own meals.

Home cooked food is inexpensive and also healthy, because you know what is best for you. You can buy vegetables in bulk, store them in the freezer, and prepare meals as per your requirements.

So, why not save some money by opting for home cooked meals most of the time.

31) In one go, try to prepare for 2 meals.

For example - For the same dish, you can just double the amount of food being cooked, in order to prepare for 2 nights dinner. Use half the quantity for one dinner and refrigerate the other half for next day's dinner.

In this way, you can prepare 2 meals at the same time and the wastage would also be less. Furthermore, you would also be saving some time, as you do not have to prepare dinner the following evening.

32) Rent out extra space in your house.

If you have an extra room in your house (which you generally use for guests), then you can also explore the opportunity to rent it out. There are sites like Airbnb.com, where you can register and can earn some extra income. After all, extra money earned is money saved. You only have to maintain the room in good condition, and then, count the money coming in.

33) Consider relocating to a place/city,

where the living costs are less than your present place of residence. You can check on internet, regarding the living costs in other cities. If any of your friends/relatives live in other cities, then you can enquire about the cost of living in those cities and do a comparison with the costs in your city. If you find a considerable difference and consequently potential savings in relocating to the other city, then you can accordingly plan to move there, for the long term. Do consider the fact that this involves a lot of pre-planning, like finding the right job, finding the right place to live and a lot of other factors.

34) You can even consider **buying/moving into a smaller house**, and putting the extra money in bank deposits/other Investments. Again, this involves a lot of pre-planning. In case you are able to get a good price for your existing house, and also, are able to get a good deal on a smaller house, then you can use the profits to invest/save as per your requirements.

35) If you have space in your house, then consider making a small garden and enjoy inexpensive, home grown, healthy vegetables. Growing vegetables in your own yard is cheaper than buying them from the market, and thus you can save some money.

36) Learn a New Skill.

Learning a new skill will add to your practical knowledge and you would be self-sufficient to do minor work by yourself, without depending on anyone else. You can take coaching for various skills as per your interest, For example - Stitching, Painting, doing Minor electrical and plumbing repair work around the house.

If you can do minor household stuff by yourself, then there is no need to pay for some external help. Thus, you can save a lot of money over time.

37) Do You Like Reading?

Why not utilize the local library, for reading Books, Journals,

Magazines, etc., instead of purchasing them?

38) Do You Like Socializing?

You can volunteer at local cultural festivals, events, exhibitions etc.

As a volunteer, you would be allowed free admissions, and related benefits, and alongside, you can also enjoy the events/exhibitions for free.

An added benefit is that you would get to meet new people and expand your circle of friends.

39) For Giving gifts during holidays/birthdays/anniversaries, set a limit on the maximum amount for which you can purchase gifts. In this way, every month, you can allocate a specified amount of money, taking into consideration the functions/parties coming up in that month, and this would help to reduce your gift giving expenses.

40) Avoid Lifestyle Inflation.

If your existing car/mobile/home appliances are functioning well, and a new model has been launched in the market, then do ask yourself - "Do I really need to buy this"?

In case it is absolutely essential, then go ahead and buy it, else you can save this money for some future use.

41) Consider Buying Older Models of Electronic items.

Whenever new models are introduced in the market, then the older models are generally offered at discounts. Examples can be of - Mobiles, Computers, Televisions, etc.

So, if you are looking to save some money, as well as purchase your coveted electronic gadgets, then consider purchasing an older model. You would still be getting most of the features, which you require for your daily use.

42) In continuation of the above point, if you really want to purchase the new model - then do look out for some good offers/promotions, like - Zero Interest EMI/Buyback offers. When launching new products, companies might provide some attractive offers also. Thus you can purchase the product without putting any unnecessary strain on your pocket.

43) In continuation of the above point - **In order to save money on purchase of new gadget,** why not consider "Exchanging" your old gadget?

In this way, you can sell off your old gadget and the resale amount will be reduced from the purchase price of the new one. Thus you can save some money.

Similar transactions are generally applied for car purchases, wherein you can exchange your old car, and get its exchange price reduced from the cost of the new car.

44) Try to make one day of the week as a "No Spending Day" (Or - Spending where it is absolutely necessary). Discuss with your family and make it a free, fun day, wherein you plan - "Not to Spend" and instead use the things/avenues already available to you. The purpose should be to make the day as enjoyable as possible, without spending any money, or spending where it is absolutely essential. For example, you can:-

- Enjoy Home Cooked food, instead of going outside.

- Play some Outdoor/Indoor games.

- Watch a movie at home.

- Go out to the Beach/Park.

In this way, you would be able to enjoy the day with your family, as well as manage to reduce the spending for that particular day.

SOME TIPS TO SAVE WATER USAGE AT HOME

45) When taking a bath, close the shower when you are applying Soap/Shampoo. This will reduce the consumption of water. Similarly, do turn off the water tap while brushing your teeth and turn it on, only when required.

46) If it is possible and convenient, then try to make an arrangement to **collect Rainwater** and then you can use it for watering the lawn, washing the front yard, etc.

These small changes can help to reduce your water bill.

SAVING MONEY WHENEVER YOU ARE CALLING, - FOR LOCAL AS WELL AS FOR OVERSEAS CALLS

47) Take an Unlimited Data Plan/Internet connection and keep in touch with your friends/business contacts through communication apps like Skype, WhatsApp, etc. If your data plan is not unlimited, then sometimes, the internet bills can be too high and you would have to spend more money on phone bills.

48) For small business related conversations/messages, consider sending a short email, as compared to making an international call.

49) Check for **any promotional schemes/discounts** being offered by competing service providers. Also, look up on the internet and then check with your current service provider for any better offers.

There is a possibility that your current service provider might themselves be running some promotional offers/discount offers. You might get lucky and save some money.

50) Check if your service provider is offering any **"Special packages" for International calls,** especially for calls to certain countries, where you need to communicate regularly.

51) Especially for Business communications, you can plan to take Per-Second Billing Plans, wherein you would be charged only for the number of seconds the call connects, and not for the full minute.

For example:- If your conversation finishes in 1 minute 15 seconds, then you would be charged for only 75 seconds, instead of full 2 minutes. So, you can save a substantial sum of money in the long run.

RELATED TO HABITS

52) Focus on doing Regular Exercise.

With a Healthy Body, you don't have to worry about any unwanted medical expenses. Your trips to the doctor would be few and your expenses on medicines would be quite less. So, indirectly, exercising regularly helps you to save money.

53) Furthermore, many of exercising options are free, or quite cheap. For example:-

- Running/Jogging,

- Swimming,

- Playing any outdoor sport with friends - Tennis, Badminton, etc.

- Yoga,

- Etc.

Indulging in the above exercising options can help you to save money on Health club membership and at the same time would do wonders for your health.

54) Have a Healthy Breakfast.

It helps to fill the stomach and thus, it reduces the urge to have snacks later on in the day. So, by reducing unwanted snacking, you are able to maintain your health and can also save money at the same time.

55) Furthermore, develop the habit of eating healthy, home cooked food and snacks.

Preparing and eating meals at home would help you to save money as well as remain healthy. In case, you are fond of eating outside, then try to limit your outings to once per week. On weekends, you can go out and enjoy with your family/friends and during the week, you can eat home cooked food.

56) Keep a bottle of water handy, especially when you are traveling.

Whenever you get thirsty during traveling, then you would have to purchase a water bottle from some store. If you can take bottled water from home, then you would not need to spend money to buy it from outside. Thus you can stay hydrated as well as save money at the same time, by adopting this habit.

57) Also, Focus on drinking more Water.

a) Water is good for digestive system and skin, so you remain healthy and hydrated.

b) Additionally, when we drink water, then it reduces the urge to drink other beverages, and thus helps in saving money.

c) Furthermore, by drinking a glass of warm water, approximately half an hour before any meal, the appetite is also controlled. A person feels less hungry, so he eats less. Thus, eating moderately helps to stay slim and the expenses on eating are also reduced.

58) Do you have any Expensive habits, like Smoking? - Can you quit?

Refraining from expensive habits like smoking can be beneficial for your health as well as for your wallet. So, why not plan to quit today?

59) Another expensive habit is - Drinking.

If you like to drink, then do so in moderation. It would be good for your finances as well as for your health.

CHAPTER 2 - SAVING MONEY WHILE AT HOME/OFFICE

60) Turn off all the lights, when they are not in use.

If we leave the lights switched on, particularly when there is no one in the room, then it is in fact wastage of money as well as electricity.

So, do make sure to switch off the lights whenever you are the last person leaving the room. In this way, any unwanted expenses on electricity can be avoided and you can save money in the long run.

Also, in case you have plenty of natural sunlight coming inside the room, then turning off the lights during daytime, can also help to reduce your electric bills over a period of time.

After all, "Money saved is money earned"

61) Install Energy Efficient Bulbs, and Tube Lights in your Home/Office, wherever possible.

Although LED bulbs can cost more initially, but they consume less power, which can help you a lot in saving money on your electricity bills over the long term.

62) Avoid using AC/Heater for long periods of time, if it is really

not required.

In summers, try to go with fans, and use the air conditioner for lesser time duration, whenever possible.

Also, in winters, you can consider putting more layers of clothing to stay warm and accordingly adjust the temperature of the heater, whenever possible.

63) Explore the option of installing Solar Panels, to save on electricity costs. Like the energy efficient light bulbs, the initial cost of solar panels is more, but you would be able to save money in the long run.

64) Monitor your Electricity bills regularly and make changes in your electrical fittings/appliances as well as electric usage accordingly, in order to lower the electricity consumption.

65) Take your Lunch from Home.

In comparison to buying/ordering food from outside, bringing home cooked meal to work can help you save a lot of money.

66) For Home/Office use, always purchase High Quality Items/ Appliances from Good Manufacturers/Reputed Brands.

This is for ensuring that you save money in the long run.

For high priced items/appliances, like Refrigerators, Air Conditioners, Washing Machines etc., it is always better to purchase Good quality and Energy Efficient items from well-known Brands.

Although this is expensive initially, but they help to save money in the long run, because:-

a) The running cost of energy efficient appliances is less.

b) Products from well-known Brands are available easily, including spare parts.

c) There are less chances of Breakdown of such appliances.

d) The Service Centers are widespread. So, in case, there is any fault in the appliance, then locating the service center and getting the repairs done is quite easy.

So, in effect, purchasing high quality items/appliances from good manufactures ensures peace of mind as well as savings in the long term.

67) In Continuation of the above point, do **get your Home Appliances serviced regularly**, as per the Manufacturer's recommended schedule, in order to avoid any sudden breakdowns and the associated costs of repair.

With a planned servicing schedule, any potential problems/replacement issues can be highlighted by the repair personnel and can be taken care of, well in time. (with comparatively lesser expenses, as opposed to expenses in case of any sudden breakdown).

68) Install Voltage Stabilizers to Protect the Electrical Appliances in your house.

Although this is expensive initially, but you are assured complete peace of mind, that all of your electrical equipment's are safe, (in the event of any voltage fluctuations).

In case voltage stabilizers are not installed and some major electrical fluctuation happens, then it would be very costly to get the appliance repaired and valuable time would also be wasted.

So, this measure helps to save money in the long run.

69) If you are doing a Job, then find out all about the perks and benefits which are being offered for employees.

For example:-

- Medical Insurance Benefits,

- Personality Development sessions/seminars,

- Discounted Club Memberships,

- Discounted Magazine Subscriptions,

- Discounted Hotel Bookings/Travel Bookings (Through tie-ups with certain travel agents),

- Etc.

By making use of these benefits, one can save money in various areas.

CHAPTER 3 - RELATED TO EARNINGS, SAVINGS AND INVESTMENTS

70) **For sustained motivation and consistent efforts, it is important to choose some "Goal" to save for.**

Having a Goal will provide extra inspiration to you, to save money.

Some examples of Goals can be:-

- To Purchase a car in 6 months,

- To go on an overseas vacation,

- To Purchase own house in 5 years,

- To save for children's education,

- To save for retirement,

- Etc.

Take out some time from your regular, day-to-day activities and make a list of all the things/experiences, which you would like to have. Then, set priorities for each item, as well as the dates, when you need to have them. This list will act as a great motivator and you would be daily inspired to save/invest money for your goals.

71) Furthermore, it is important to **discuss your saving related goals** and plans with your family members, so that they can also give in their inputs.

This would also help to motivate you further, as the entire family would be working towards a common goal.

72) If required, then **have a Mentor/Financial advisor,** who can guide you regarding your finances. You can take also advice from your close friends.

Good Ideas can come at any time, from any source. So, regularly keep discussing, evaluating and implementing good advice for a better financial future.

73) Start saving as early as possible (if possible, starting with your first paycheck), and stick to your savings schedule.

It is an established fact – the earlier you start saving, the more beneficial it would be for your finances, as your wealth gets more time to get compounded over the years.

74) Set up an **Automatic Saving/Investing mechanism**.

Whenever you receive your salary,

- Make sure to transfer a small percentage of the salary to another savings/investment/a retirement account. You can discuss with your bank personnel for the procedure.

If you feel comfortable to invest, then consider starting a monthly investment plan in Mutual Funds, wherein a fixed amount of money is automatically deducted from your account every month, and invested in the funds of your choice. (But do consult your financial advisor before doing so).

These small amounts might seem insignificant at first, but over a period of time, say 3 - 4 years, you would be having a good sum of money.

75) Similarly, **when you receive any bonus/increment** at your job, do transfer a small percentage of the same, to your separate savings/investment account. These small additions to your savings account will help you to accumulate a tidy sum in the years to come.

76) Earn More to Save More.

- If it is possible, then consider taking up a second part time job, to increase your income.

- Consider starting a side business (Online/Offline, as per your interest and convenience).

The more you earn, the more opportunities you would be having, for saving money.

77) Discuss with an Accountant regarding all the possible Tax saving avenues, in order to further save, as well as to invest your money.

78) Check out the Offers and services provided by different Banks, and if convenient, open an account, where you get the maximum benefits, in terms of:-

a) Lower fees charged for various services.

b) Higher Interest provided on deposits.

c) Attractive Offers on Debit Card/Credit Card.

d) Attractive Loan facilities provided.

Etc.

79) Choose the right accounts/investments, based on your requirements and convenience.

For example:-

- A simple savings account will give less interest for your money.

- A Fixed Deposit can give more interest as compared to a simple savings account.

- Based on your risk appetite, you can start investing in Mutual Funds/Shares (But do consult your financial advisor before doing so).

80) Check, whether you are spending more money for your ATM Transactions.

Generally, banks allow a few, free transactions per month on ATM's. But after that, a fee is charged for each additional transaction.

So, if you can manage your work within the free transactions only, then you would not have to spend any extra money.

Additionally, it is better to do all the transactions online, so that the need for cash is reduced and thus, you have less ATM transactions.

81) Plan and have an Emergency Fund to cover at least 4-6 months of routine expenditures.

This is to ensure that, whenever you need some money for any unplanned expenses, then you do not have to take it out from your regular savings/fixed deposits.

82) Always have adequate Insurance. For example:-

- Health Insurance,

- Vehicle Insurance,

- House insurance,

- Travel insurance,

- Etc.

With Insurance, you have peace of mind. And in case of any unfortunate circumstances, you do not have to dip into your savings and spend the entire amount yourself. Thus, having insurance will help you to save money, as the insurance company would take care of most of the expenses.

83) Also, before renewing the insurance policies, check out the latest offers and deals from other companies also. They might be having some Promotional offers/Discounts/Extra services and you might be able to save some money on renewals.

84) If you invest in Mutual Funds, then consider investing in "Direct plans" of mutual funds, where the expenses are lower as compared to regular plans. You would notice an appreciable increase in the size of your investments in the long term.

85) Similarly, when investing directly in Shares, find a broker, who charges the lowest commission. This would also help you save money.

Some brokers charge Zero commission for Delivery based orders, and only charge for Intraday trades. So, in case you want to buy and hold shares for the long term, then it can save you a lot of money in broker commissions.

The most important thing is to consult your financial advisor, before making any kind of investments in shares/mutual funds.

CHAPTER 4 – RELATED TO DEBT, LOANS, CREDIT CARDS

86) Get Out of any Existing Debt ASAP.

It might be:-

- The Home loan,

- The Car Loan,

- Personal Loan,

- Student Loan/Educational loan,

- Credit Card Debt,

- Etc.

When too much debt piles up, then our focus gets shifted from saving, and instead we start concentrating on servicing the debt and paying the monthly interest and the installments.

So, make it an "Absolute Necessity" to get out of debt, as soon as possible.

- Make a list of all the areas where you have a loan.

- Then organize all those areas by priority.

- Start working to remove those points one by one. As per your convenience, you can take up an additional, part-time job in order to earn more money, or even dip into your existing savings, in order to clear off the existing debt.

Paying off all your loans at the earliest will help a lot in saving extra money in the long term.

87) Avoid having New Debt.

Wherever possible, try to avoid taking on new debt, till the previous one is taken care of.

Also, if you financial situation allows, then try to purchase with upfront payment. Thus, you will not have to worry about interest payments.

CHAPTER 5 - WHEN PARTYING/GOING OUT FOR ENTERTAINMENT

88) Do try out Inexpensive ways for Entertainment/Leisure, like:-

- Going to the Park with family/friends.

- Going to the beach.

- Going out for a picnic.

- Bike riding trips.

- Playing some outdoor/indoor sports.

As the saying goes-"Some of the best things in life are free", so why not enjoy the free stuff.

89) Develop some Hobby, which can also help you to save money. For example:-

- Gardening - (You can save money in comparison to paying salary to the gardener).

- Arts and Crafts (For gifting purposes, you can yourself make gifts and presents at home, instead of buying from outside).

- Learn Sewing (In this way, you can repair your clothes yourself instead of paying to the tailor/buying new clothes).

90) Plan a "Get together" with your friends at home only, instead of going out.

Each person can prepare a dish at his/her home and then, they can all get together at the house party and enjoy healthy home-cooked food. Thus, everyone can remain within their budget and can save money.

Furthermore, you can all watch movies, play games and do a lot of other interesting stuff at home, instead of going out.

91) Subscribe to the Email newsletters of the cinema halls.

In this way, you would receive notifications about new movie releases, as well as any special, discounted offers.

Also, download and install some good movie ticket booking apps on your mobile, so that you are notified of new releases as well as any promotional offers.

92) Whenever you plan to go outside for work/leisure, "Eat something before going out of home".

In this way, you would be feeling full, and thus, the chances of spending money on food and drinks outside are reduced.

93) Whenever you spend on "Indulgences" (like a dinner at an expensive restaurant), then try to put in the same amount of money in your separate savings/investment account. This will work wonders for your savings in the long run.

94) Ask for Discounts.

Whenever you are going out for movies, concerts, entertainment parks etc., while purchasing tickets, - Do ask, if they offer any discounts for students, seniors, etc. They might be offering some discounts/having some special offers and you might get lucky and save some money.

95) Some Restaurants/Fast Food outlets might be offering "Best Value Meals", which can help you save money. Do check out those deals. Some might also be offering discounts on packed food, whereas some might be offering free home deliveries, etc. So, do explore the various options available.

96) In case, you have a get together and everyone wants to order restaurant food, (and are not in the mood to cook themselves, or simply do not have the time), then consider installing food delivery apps in your mobile and check if there are any promotional offers going on. You might be able to save some money on restaurant food in this way.

CHAPTER 6 - RELATED TO VEHICLES/ TRANSPORTATION

MONEY SAVING TIPS WHILE BUYING A NEW CAR

97) When you are planning to purchase a new car, in addition to checking the prices of the new cars, check out the prices of used cars also. You might be able to get all the features you require, within your budget.

98) Shop Around. Go to various dealerships to check the various car models and prices, which are in your budget. In this way, you would be having a lot of options to choose from and can then decide upon the best option.

99) Also, do check online for car features and prices, from various websites. Some deals might only be available online. So, it might help you a lot.

100) When you have finalized on the particular car model and the dealership, then start **"Negotiating"** for the car price and the prices of accessories.

101) Additionally, do also negotiate for the Insurance charges, Initial free services as well as the warranty terms and conditions.

102) Opt for Full/Comprehensive Insurance and Extended Warranty for your car.

The car manufacturers provide a regular warranty period for the new vehicle and they also provide option to the customer to purchase the extended warranty.

One should purchase the extended warranty also. Though this option looks expensive in the beginning, but you are assured complete peace of mind.

For example - In case there is any issue with the engine/any other car part, during the warranty period, then you do not have to pay anything. The company takes care of that, as it is under the normal/extended warranty.

Also, one should opt for comprehensive insurance for the vehicle. (In case, the car gets damaged in an accident, then you do not have to suffer any unnecessary financial loss, as the car is insured).

Thus, these options help you to save money in the long run.

103) Whenever purchasing any vehicle, make sure that it is "Fuel Efficient". You would not want to spend a major portion of your money on fuel costs only.

You can check regarding the fuel efficiency from various sources, like:-

- Dealerships.

- Reviews in Automobile Magazines.

- Your friends/relatives, in case anyone has that particular car already. They can share their ownership experience with you and then, you can take your decision accordingly.

104) For better fuel efficiency, drive in the speed range, which has been recommended by the car manufacturer.

Car manufacturers perform extensive tests on the car models to arrive at the speed range, which provides the best fuel efficiency. So following their recommendations can help you save money on fuel. Do check out the car's manual for these details.

GENERAL MONEY SAVING TIPS FOR VEHICLES/ TRANSPORTATION

105) Shop Around for Latest Deals on Car Insurance.

Before the car's insurance renewal is due, look out for offers from various other service providers also. Get renewal quotes from them, and check all the details.

Once you find a good deal, then either you can re-negotiate with your existing insurance provider, or you can go ahead with the new service provider.

106) Get your Car/Bike Serviced Regularly.

It is necessary to follow the manufacturer's recommendations and get your vehicles serviced at scheduled intervals. All the servicing details are mentioned in the vehicle's manual.

In this way, you can avoid sudden breakdowns and the associated costs of repair.

Thus, adhering to preventive maintenance schedules helps in saving money in the long run.

107) Learning the minor things about your vehicle can also help

you save money.

For example - If you know how to fix the puncture of a "Tubeless tire", then you don't have to pay someone else to do it for you. Also, if you can learn how to check the engine oil, and top it up (if required), then you do not have to go to the service center every time. Similarly, you can also learn to check the battery connections etc.

108) Try Carpooling.

If a few people from the same neighborhood are going in the same direction, then all of them can plan to go in one car, thus reducing the fuel expenses, as well as the maintenance expense for the vehicles. You also have the benefit of having some company along the way.

You can even fix the days, when each person uses his/her car, and the fuel expenses can be shared accordingly.

At office also, you can discuss with your colleagues, and if there a possibility of picking some people on the way to office and dropping them on the way back, then everyone can contribute to the fuel costs and can thus save money.

109) Install "Taxi booking apps" on your phone, and make use of them, as required.

You should calculate the economics of using these apps vis-à-vis the cost of using your own car, and then decide as per suitability and convenience.

A small example can be - When one travels by his own car, then he has to spend time looking for a parking space and pay the parking fees, and then walk towards his office, whereas when one goes by taxi, then he can reach directly at the front door of his office/factory.

Furthermore, sometimes these apps might also have some good

promotions, which can help you to save money. You can check for offers from competing apps and decide accordingly.

110) Similarly, you can consider taking "Public transportation" (Bus/Metro), wherever possible. For example, if there is a metro station close to your home, and also a metro station close to your office, then you can consider taking a metro to your office, instead of going by your own car.

It proves to be cheaper as compared to taking your own vehicle, and you also don't have to worry about driving through traffic jams, flat tires, parking, fuel expenses, etc.

111) Purchase a Weekly/Monthly Pass.

When using public transportation, instead of buying tickets daily, explore the option of purchasing a weekly/monthly pass. In this way, your cost per trip would be reduced, thus saving you money. Furthermore, there would be an additional benefit that you would not have to wait in line every day to purchase the ticket. So, it saves some time as well.

112) Is your office close to your home? Can you explore the option of walking/cycling to work?

In addition to being beneficial for your Health, walking/cycling can also help you to save some serious money, (especially when compared to "going by car", wherein you have to take into account fuel costs, parking, flat tires and the added stress of heavy traffic jams).

CHAPTER 7 – SAVING MONEY WHILE TRAVELLING/GOING ON A VACATION

SAVING MONEY WHILE BOOKING HOTELS AND FLIGHT TICKETS

113) Plan your travel/vacations in advance (wherever possible), so that you are able to get the best as well as discounted deals on tickets, hotel bookings etc. Generally, the earlier you book, the better prices you can get. So, you can save some money by planning your travels in advance.

114) Check out the prices from various Travel agents, as well as Online, in order to get the best deals on travel tickets as well as on hotels.

115) If it is possible, then plan your travels/vacation in the off-season.

There are more chances of getting substantial discounts on airline tickets, hotel bookings, if you travel in the off-season.

An additional benefit is that, the tourist places are not much crowded during the off-season.

116) Also, try to be flexible in your schedule (both for vacations as well as for business travel). If you can shift your travel dates by a few days here and there, then you can get some better price options, both for tickets, as well as for hotel rooms.

117) If the options are available, then go for "Refundable" air tickets as well as refundable hotel bookings.

In case, for any reason, you need to change your travel dates, then your loss would be reduced with a refundable ticket.

Whereas, if you purchase a non-refundable ticket and due to any reason, you have to cancel it, then it would be a total loss of the ticket price.

118) Whenever you book hotels, do check whether the following facilities are available:-

- Complimentary Breakfast.

- Complimentary Airport pickup/Drop off facilities.

- Complimentary Internet/Wi-Fi in room.

- Complimentary use of Gym and Swimming pool.

Generally, hotels might provide some/all of the above facilities to their guests. So, you do not have to spend any extra money.

119) In case the Hotel is not offering free pick-up from the airport, then do explore the other economical options available, like- Shuttle Buses, Metro, Shared Taxis etc.

120) Whenever you stay in a hotel, do enquire if they have some **"Membership Options"** for their hotel chain and subscribe for the same.

In this way, you would be notified of any special offers/discounts during a certain period and thus, you can plan your holidays accordingly.

121) Explore the local cuisine of the city, where you are travel-

ling.

Local food outlets/fast food chains are generally inexpensive and you also get to enjoy the local food.

122) If you are going to travel between cities, then do purchase a "Rail pass", so that you can travel from one city to another, quite conveniently and economically. You can purchase these rail passes online and after that, you just need to check the train time tables. You do not have to stand in queues to purchase the rail ticket. You can just reach the station some time earlier and board the train. Thus, apart from saving money, you also save time during your trip.

123) Get an "International Prepaid SIM card", before leaving your home country, or else, get a mobile connection, when you reach your destination country.

Getting a connection is important, because making local/international calls from hotels can be quite expensive.

Nowadays, you can get a lot of options from various service providers, who can provide you with doorstep delivery of sim card, along with competitive calling rates, even before you leave your home country. In this way, whenever you land in your destination country, you do not have to go to the shopping malls/mobile shops, especially to purchase the sim card.

Thus, getting a sim card before travelling, is convenient as well as a money saving option.

124) Also, you can make use of the free Wi-Fi available at hotels, coffee shops, restaurants etc., in order to save money on internet bills. Sometimes, the data plans on your sim card may be quite expensive. So, whenever you go out for coffee/food, then you can use the complementary Wi-Fi available there.

125) In case you travel a lot, either for vacations or for business purposes, then opt for the "Annual Travel insurance plans". Although these look expensive initially, but they will help you to save money throughout the year, as you do not have to purchase travel insurance for each trip separately. So, ultimately, the insurance cost per trip comes down.

ENDING FOR NOW

"Thank you" for Reading this Book.

Before you go. I would like to say "Thank you" for reading this book.

I hope that you have enjoyed reading this short book, and have been able to get some ideas on how to develop the habit of saving money in various walks of life.

I know that everyone is busy, especially you, and i know that you could have picked from a wide variety of books on this topic, but you took a chance with my book.

So, a BIG "Thank you", - For downloading this book and reading it all the way towards the end.

CAN I ASK A SMALL FAVOR?

Could you please take a minute or two and leave a Review for this book on Amazon?

I would appreciate the Feedback. I personally read all the reviews and your Feedback would help me to improve my upcoming books and to continue writing the kind of books that readers find entertaining and informative.

And if you liked this book, then please let me know.

Thank you.

ROCKY KUMAR

www.PassionateIdeas.net

WOULD YOU LIKE TO GET THE LATEST INFORMATION ABOUT MY NEW AND UPCOMING RELEASES?

I write about Productivity and Financial Habits, and am currently in the process of finalizing a couple of more books for publishing.

You can click the link given below, to SUBSCRIBE to my Blog, and get timely updates on future book releases.

Happy Reading.....

ROCKY KUMAR.

Subscribe for Updates at:- www.PassionateIdeas.net

ABOUT THE AUTHOR

ROCKY KUMAR is an Explorer at Heart. He loves travelling around the world, exploring new places, experiences and things.

He likes Teaching and Offering Consultancy Services to Business Establishments and is always looking for Good Ideas and Opportunities for Personal as well as for Professional Growth.

He also loves to write about Productivity & Finance and is in the process of finalizing more Exciting Books in the times to come.

You can Subscribe for Updates at:-

www.PassionateIdeas.net

www.ingramcontent.com/pod-product-compliance
Lightning Source LLC
Chambersburg PA
CBHW070824220526
45466CB00002B/755